Salads

Salads

Jane Price

MURDOCH BOOKS

contents

tossed

The acclaimed French chef Alexis Soyer hypothetically asked if there were anything 'more refreshing than salads when your appetite seems to have deserted you?'.

Cooks and diners have embraced a veritable world of salads bursting with bright, tangy flavors, wondrous textures, and an array of fresh ingredients. Of course we all still love the classics—potato salad, bean salad, and coleslaw, for example. But it's been nothing short of a gastronomic epiphany to delve into the vegetable crisper, the deli, and other cuisines, to realize that salad combinations such as orange, goat's cheese, and hazelnut, or watercress, feta, and watermelon are delicious possibilities.

We've taken cues from Morocco and tossed carrots with olives and mint, and from Thailand we have tasty noodle salads. Salad boredom is forever banished with the chargrilling of cauliflower, the roasting of tomatoes, and the serving of potato salad warm, slathered in a tasty green olive dressing.

Salads can be light, complementing a main course or they can serve as an appetite-teasing starter. Salads can also be substantial meals in their own right, based around generous servings of meat, tofu, or seafood. They can be dressed with the simplest dash of oil and vinegar, homemade mayonnaise, or special vinaigrettes. Whether humble and homey, sophisticated, comforting and familiar, or thrillingly foreign, there's a salad recipe here for any and every occasion you could possibly imagine.

classic

Caesar salad

3 eggs
3 garlic cloves, crushed
2–3 anchovy fillets
1 teaspoon worcestershire sauce
2 tablespoons lime juice
1 teaspoon dijon mustard
¾ cup olive oil
3 slices white bread
½ oz butter
1 tablespoon olive oil, extra
3 bacon slices
1 large or 4 baby romaine lettuces
¾ cup shaved parmesan cheese

Process the eggs, garlic, anchovies, worcestershire sauce, lime juice, and mustard in a food processor until smooth. With the motor running, add the oil in a thin, continuous stream to produce a creamy dressing. Season to taste.

Cut the crusts off the bread, then cut the bread into ½-inch cubes.

Heat the butter and extra olive oil in a frying pan over medium heat. Add the bread and cook for 5–8 minutes, or until crisp, then remove from the pan. Cook the bacon in the pan for 3 minutes, or until crisp, then break into bite-sized pieces.

Toss the romaine lettuce leaves with the dressing, then add the croutons and bacon and top with the parmesan cheese.

SERVES 4–6

Green salad with lemon vinaigrette

5½ oz baby romaine lettuce
5½ oz small butter lettuce
1¾ oz watercress
3½ oz arugula
1 tablespoon finely chopped shallots
2 teaspoons dijon mustard
½ teaspoon sugar
1 tablespoon finely chopped basil
1 teaspoon grated lemon zest
3 teaspoons lemon juice
1 tablespoon white wine vinegar
1 fl oz lemon oil
2½ fl oz extra virgin olive oil

Remove the outer leaves from the romaine and butter lettuces and separate the core leaves. Wash in cold water, place in a colander to drain, then refrigerate. Pinch or trim the stalks from the watercress and arugula. Pat dry and chill with the lettuce.

To make the dressing, whisk together the shallot, mustard, sugar, basil, lemon zest, lemon juice, and vinegar in a bowl until well blended. Place the oils in a small jug and slowly add to the bowl in a thin stream, whisking constantly to create a smooth, creamy dressing. Season to taste.

Put the salad greens in a large bowl. Drizzle the dressing over the salad and toss gently to coat.

SERVES 6

Panzanella

7 oz ciabatta bread
8 firm vine-ripened tomatoes
4 tablespoons olive oil
1 tablespoon lemon juice
1½ tablespoons red wine vinegar
6 anchovy fillets, finely chopped
1 tablespoon baby capers, rinsed, squeezed dry
  and finely chopped
1 garlic clove, crushed
1 oz basil leaves

Preheat the oven to 425°F. Tear the bread into ¾-inch cubes. Spread on a baking sheet and bake for 5–7 minutes, or until golden. Leave the toasted bread on a wire rack to cool.

Score a cross in the base of each tomato. Place in a heatproof bowl and cover with boiling water. Leave for 30 seconds, then transfer to cold water and peel the skin away from the cross. Cut four of the tomatoes in half and squeeze the juice and seeds into a bowl, reserving and chopping the flesh. Add the oil, juice, vinegar, anchovies, capers, and garlic to the tomato juice and season.

Seed and slice the remaining tomatoes, and place in a large bowl with the reserved tomato and most of the basil. Add the dressing and toasted bread, and toss. Garnish with the remaining basil, season, and leave for at least 15 minutes. Serve at room temperature.

SERVES 6

NOTE: This salad is also known as Tuscan bread salad.

Greek salad

4 firm, ripe tomatoes, cut into wedges
1 large cucumber, peeled, halved,
    seeded and cut into small cubes
2 green peppers, seeded, halved
    lengthways, and cut into strips
1 red onion, finely sliced
16 Kalamata olives
1¾ cup cubed firm feta cheese
1 small handful Italian parsley
12 mint leaves
½ cup olive oil
2 tablespoons lemon juice
1 garlic clove, crushed

Put the tomato, cucumber, pepper, onion, olives, feta, and half the parsley and mint leaves in a large salad bowl and gently mix together.

Put the oil, lemon juice, and garlic in a screwtop jar, season and shake until combined. Pour the dressing over the salad and toss lightly. Garnish with the remaining parsley and mint.

SERVES 4

Coleslaw

½ green cabbage
¼ red cabbage
3 carrots, coarsely grated
6 radishes, coarsely grated
1 red pepper, chopped
4 scallions, sliced
½ cup chopped Italian parsley
1 cup mayonnaise

Remove the hard core from the cabbages and shred the leaves with a sharp knife. Put in a large bowl and add the carrot, radish, pepper, scallion, and parsley to the bowl.

Add the mayonnaise, season to taste and toss until well combined.

SERVES 8–10

NOTE: Cover and refrigerate the chopped vegetables for up to 3 hours before serving. Add the mayonnaise just before serving.

Dill potato salad

1 lb 5 oz waxy red-skinned potatoes
2 eggs
2 tablespoons finely chopped dill
1½ tablespoons finely chopped shallots
1 egg yolk
2 teaspoons lemon juice
1 teaspoon dijon mustard
3½ fl oz light olive oil

Bring a large saucepan of water to a boil. Cook the potatoes for 20 minutes, or until tender. Add the eggs for the last 10 minutes. Remove the potatoes and eggs, and allow to cool.

Peel the potatoes, then cut into ¾- –1¼-inch cubes. Peel and chop the eggs. Place the potato in a large bowl with the dill, eggs, and shallot. Toss to combine, then season.

Process the egg yolk, lemon juice, mustard, and a pinch of salt in a food processor. With the motor running, gradually add the olive oil a few drops at a time. When about half the oil has been added, pour in the remaining oil in a steady stream until it has all been incorporated. Use a large metal spoon to gently combine the potato and mayonnaise, then serve.

SERVES 4

Salad Niçoise

3 tablespoons lemon juice
1 garlic clove, crushed
5 fl oz olive oil
14 oz waxy potatoes, such as
   Charlotte or fingerling
3 eggs
4 oz green beans, trimmed
1 green pepper, seeded
   and sliced
4 oz black olives

2 firm, ripe tomatoes, cut into
   wedges
1 small cucumber, cut into
   chunks
3 scallions, cut into ¾-inch
   lengths
3 fresh tuna steaks

Put the lemon juice, garlic, and 4 fl oz of the olive oil in a jar with a screw-top lid. Season and shake the jar well to combine.

Boil the potatoes in a saucepan of salted water for 10–12 minutes, or until tender. Add the eggs for the final 8 minutes of cooking. Drain, cool the eggs under cold water, then peel and quarter. Cool the potatoes, then cut into chunks. Bring a saucepan of salted water to a boil, add the green beans and blanch for 3 minutes. Drain and refresh under cold water. Drain well, then slice in half on the diagonal.

Put the potato and beans in a large bowl, and add the pepper, olives, tomato, cucumber, and scallion. Strain the garlic from the dressing. Pour half over the salad, toss and transfer to a serving dish.

Heat a frying pan over very high heat. Add the remaining olive oil. Season the tuna steaks and cook for 2 minutes on each side, or until rare. Allow to cool for 5 minutes, then slice thinly. Arrange on top of the salad with the eggs, and drizzle with the remaining dressing.

SERVES 4

Egg salad with creamy dressing

10 large eggs, at room
   temperature
1 egg yolk
3 teaspoons lemon juice
2 teaspoons dijon mustard
2½ fl oz olive oil
2½ fl oz safflower oil

2 tablespoons chopped dill
1 fl oz crème fraîche or sour
   cream
2 tablespoons baby capers,
   squeezed dry and drained
1 cup mustard cress

Put the eggs in a large saucepan of cold water. Bring to a boil and simmer gently for 10 minutes. Drain, then cool the eggs under cold running water. Remove the shells.

Place the egg yolk, lemon juice, and dijon mustard in a food processor or blender and season. With the motor running, slowly add the combined olive oil and safflower oil, drop by drop at first, then slowly increasing the amount to a thin, steady stream as the mixture thickens. When all of the oil has been added, put the mayonnaise in a large bowl and gently stir in the dill, crème fraîche, and capers.

Roughly chop the eggs and fold into the mayonnaise. Transfer the salad to a serving bowl and use scissors to cut the green tips from the mustard cress. Scatter over the salad and serve.

SERVES 4

Tabbouleh

¾ cup bulgur
3 firm, ripe tomatoes
1 large cucumber
4 scallions, sliced
4 cups chopped Italian parsley
½ cup chopped mint

Dressing
4 tablespoons lemon juice
3 tablespoons olive oil
1 tablespoon extra virgin olive oil

Place the bulgur in a bowl, cover with 2 cups water and leave for 1½ hours.

Cut the tomatoes in half, squeeze to remove any excess seeds and cut into ½-inch cubes. Cut the cucumber in half lengthways, remove the seeds with a teaspoon and cut the flesh into ½-inch cubes.

To make the dressing, place the lemon juice and 1½ teaspoons salt in a bowl and whisk until well combined. Season well with freshly ground black pepper and slowly whisk in the olive oil and extra virgin olive oil.

Drain the bulgur and squeeze out any excess water. Spread the bulgur out on paper towel and leave to dry for about 30 minutes. Put the bulgur in a large salad bowl, add the tomato, cucumber, scallion, parsley, and mint, and toss well to combine. Pour the dressing over the salad and toss until evenly coated.

SERVES 6

Fattoush

2 pita bread rounds
6 romaine lettuce leaves, shredded
1 large cucumber, cubed
4 firm, ripe tomatoes, cut into ¾-inch cubes
8 scallions, chopped
4 tablespoons finely chopped Italian parsley
1 tablespoon finely chopped mint
2 tablespoons finely chopped cilantro leaves

Dressing
2 garlic cloves, crushed
3½ fl oz extra virgin olive oil
3½ fl oz lemon juice

Preheat the oven to 350°F. Split the bread in half through the center and bake on a baking tray for 8–10 minutes, or until golden and crisp, turning halfway through. Break into pieces.

To make the dressing, whisk all the ingredients together in a bowl until well combined.

Place the bread and remaining salad ingredients in a serving bowl and toss to combine. Drizzle with the dressing and toss well. Season to taste. Serve immediately.

SERVES 6

Insalata caprese

3 large vine-ripened tomatoes
9 oz bocconcini
12 basil leaves
3 tablespoons extra virgin olive oil
4 basil leaves, extra, roughly torn

Slice the tomato into twelve ½-inch thick slices. Slice the bocconcini into 24 slices the same thickness as the tomato.

Arrange the tomato slices on a plate, alternating them with 2 slices of bocconcini and placing a basil leaf between the bocconcini slices.

Drizzle with the olive oil, sprinkle with the torn basil and season well.

SERVES 4

starters

Chargrilled
vegetable salad

4 baby eggplants
5 firm, ripe plum tomatoes
2 red peppers
1 green pepper
2 zucchini
3½ fl oz olive oil
12 bocconcini
3 tablespoons Ligurian olives
1 garlic clove, finely chopped
3 teaspoons baby capers, rinsed and squeezed dry
½ teaspoon sugar
2 tablespoons balsamic vinegar

Cut the eggplants and tomatoes in half lengthways. Cut the red and green peppers in half lengthways, remove the seeds and membrane then cut each half into 3 pieces. Thinly slice the zucchini on the diagonal.

Preheat a chargrill pan or barbecue hotplate over medium heat. Add 1 tablespoon of oil and cook a quarter of the vegetables (cook the tomatoes cut side down first) for about 2–3 minutes, or until it is golden and grill marks appear. Put in a bowl.

Cook the remaining vegetables in batches until tender, adding more oil as needed. Transfer to the bowl and add the baby bocconcini. Mix the olives, garlic, capers, sugar, vinegar, and remaining oil (about 2 tablespoons). Pour over the salad and toss. Season with pepper.

SERVES 4–6

Asparagus
orange salad

10½ oz thin, fresh asparagus spears
1⅔ cups watercress
½ small red onion, very thinly sliced
1 orange, cut into 12 segments
1 tablespoon fresh orange juice
1 teaspoon finely grated orange zest
1 teaspoon sugar
1 tablespoon red wine vinegar
2 teaspoons poppy seeds
2 tablespoons olive oil
2¼ oz soft goat's cheese

Cook the asparagus in boiling water for 1–2 minutes, or until just tender. Rinse under cold water to cool.

Combine the asparagus with the watercress, red onion, and orange segments on a serving platter.

Combine the orange juice, orange zest, sugar, vinegar, and poppy seeds in a cup. Whisk in the oil with a fork until combined and drizzle over the salad. Crumble the goat's cheese over the salad and season to taste.

SERVES 4

Frisée and garlic crouton salad

Vinaigrette
1 shallot, finely chopped
1 tablespoon dijon mustard
3 tablespoons tarragon vinegar
2/3 cup extra virgin olive oil

1 tablespoon olive oil
1/2 bread stick, sliced
4 garlic cloves
1 baby curly endive, washed and dried
1 cup walnuts, toasted
2/3 cup crumbled feta cheese

To make the vinaigrette, whisk together the shallot, mustard, and vinegar in a bowl. Slowly add the oil, whisking constantly until thickened. Set aside.

Heat the oil in a large frying pan over medium–high heat. Add the bread and garlic and cook for 5–8 minutes, or until the croutons are crisp. Remove the garlic from the pan. Once the croutons are cool, break into small pieces.

Place the endive, croutons, walnuts, feta cheese, and vinaigrette in a large bowl. Toss together well and serve.

SERVES 4–6

Bacon and avocado salad

8 bacon slices
14 oz green beans, topped, tailed and halved
10½ oz baby spinach leaves
2 shallots, finely sliced
2 ripe avocados
¼ teaspoon brown sugar
1 garlic clove, crushed
4 tablespoons olive oil
1 tablespoon balsamic vinegar
1 teaspoon sesame oil

Preheat the broiler. Put the bacon on a tray and broil on both sides until crisp. Leave to cool, then break into pieces.

Bring a saucepan of water to a boil and cook the beans for 4 minutes. Drain and rinse under cold running water for a few seconds.

Put the spinach in a large bowl and add the beans, bacon, and shallot. Halve the avocados, then cut into cubes and add to the bowl.

Mix the brown sugar and garlic in a small bowl. Add the remaining ingredients and whisk together.

Pour the dressing over the salad and toss well. Season before serving.

SERVES 4

Smoked salmon
and arugula salad

Dressing
2 tablespoons extra virgin olive oil
1 tablespoon balsamic vinegar

5½ oz arugula leaves
1 ripe avocado
9 oz smoked salmon slices
11½ oz marinated goat's cheese, drained and crumbled
2 tablespoons roasted hazelnuts, roughly chopped

Fish substitution
smoked trout

To make the dressing, thoroughly whisk together the oil and vinegar in a bowl. Season to taste.

Trim the long stems from the arugula. Rinse the leaves, pat dry and gently toss in a bowl with the dressing.

Cut the avocado into wedges. Put about three wedges on each serving plate with the salmon and arugula. Scatter the cheese and nuts over the top and season with freshly ground black pepper.

SERVES 4

Fava bean, mint, and bacon salad

1 lb 5 oz frozen fava beans (see Notes)
1 butter or romaine lettuce, shredded (about 5½ oz)
¾ cup shredded mint
9 oz piece Kasseler or pancetta (see Notes)
1 tablespoon olive oil

1½ teaspoons dijon mustard
1 teaspoon sugar
2 tablespoons white wine vinegar
3 tablespoons extra virgin olive oil
4 pita bread rounds

Blanch the beans, according to the packet instructions. Drain, rinse under cold water, and peel. Place in a large bowl with the lettuce and mint.

Slice the Kasseler into thick slices, then into ¾-inch chunks. Heat the oil in a heavy-based frying pan and cook the Kasseler for 3–4 minutes, or until golden. Add to the bean mixture.

Combine the mustard, sugar, and vinegar in a cup. Whisk in the oil until well combined and season. Pile the salad onto fresh or lightly toasted pita breads to serve.

SERVES 4

NOTES: If they are in season, you may like to use fresh fava beans. You will need about 4 lbs beans in the pod to give 1 lb 5 oz beans. Boil the beans for 2 minutes and peel before using them.

Kasseler is a traditional German specialty. It is a cured and smoked loin of pork that comes in a single piece and should be available at good delicatessens.

Avocado and grapefruit salad

2 ruby grapefruit
1 ripe avocado
7 oz watercress
1 shallot, finely sliced
1 tablespoon sherry vinegar
3 tablespoons olive oil

Peel and segment the grapefruit, working over a bowl to save any juice drips for the dressing.

Cut the avocado into ¾-inch thick wedges and put in a bowl with the watercress, grapefruit, and shallot.

Put 1 tablespoon of the reserved grapefruit juice in a small, screw-top jar with the vinegar, oil, salt, and black pepper, and shake well. Pour the dressing over the salad and toss gently.

SERVES 4

Orange and goat's cheese salad

¾ oz hazelnuts
1 tablespoon orange juice
1 tablespoon lemon juice
½ cup olive oil
9 oz watercress

1 cup baby spinach leaves
24 orange segments
10½ oz firm goat's cheese,
    sliced into 4 equal portions

Preheat the oven to 350°F. Put the hazelnuts on a tray and roast for 5–6 minutes, or until the skin turns dark brown. Wrap the hazelnuts in a dish cloth and rub together to remove the skins.

Combine the nuts, orange juice, lemon juice, and a pinch of salt in a food processor. With the motor running, gradually add the oil a few drops at a time. When about half the oil has been added, pour in the remainder in a steady stream.

Remove the stems from the watercress and put the leaves in a bowl with the spinach, orange segments, and 2 tablespoons of the dressing. Toss to combine and season to taste with pepper. Arrange the salad on four plates.

Heat a small, non-stick frying pan over medium–high heat and brush lightly with olive oil. When hot, carefully press each slice of goat's cheese firmly into the pan and cook for 1–2 minutes, or until a crust has formed on the cheese. Carefully remove the cheese from the pan and arrange over the salads, crust-side-up. Drizzle the remaining dressing over the salads.

SERVES 4

Pear and walnut salad

Dressing
3½ oz creamy blue cheese
3 tablespoons olive oil
1 tablespoon walnut oil
1 tablespoon lemon juice
1 tablespoon cream
2 teaspoons finely chopped sage

1 cup walnut halves
4 firm, ripe small pears
2 tablespoons lemon juice
2 heads Belgian endive, trimmed
    and leaves separated
1 cup parmesan cheese, shaved

To make the dressing, purée the blue cheese in a small processor, then add the olive oil, walnut oil, and lemon juice, and blend until smooth. With the motor running, slowly add 2 teaspoons of warm water. Stir in the cream and sage and season to taste.

Preheat the broiler. Put the walnuts in a bowl and cover with boiling water. Allow to soak for 1 minute, then drain. Spread the walnuts on a baking tray and place under the broiler for 3 minutes, or until lightly toasted. Chop coarsely.

Thinly slice across the pears through the core to make rounds. Do not peel or core the pears, but discard the seeds. As each pear is sliced, sprinkle with a little lemon juice to prevent discoloration. On each serving plate, arrange three pear slices in a circle.

Top with a scattering of walnuts, a couple of endive leaves, a few more walnuts, and some parmesan. Repeat this layering, reserving the last layer of parmesan and some of the walnuts. Spoon some dressing over each stack, scatter with the remaining walnuts, and top with the reserved parmesan.

SERVES 4

Mixed salad with warm Brie dressing

½ sourdough baguette
5½ fl oz extra virgin olive oil
6 bacon slices
2 garlic cloves, peeled
2 baby romaine lettuce
1¾ cups baby spinach leaves
½ cup pine nuts, toasted
2 shallots, finely chopped

1 tablespoon dijon mustard
4 tablespoons sherry vinegar
10½ oz ripe Brie cheese, rind removed

Preheat the oven to 350°F. Thinly slice the baguette on the diagonal.

Use 2 tablespoons of oil to brush both sides of each slice, place on a baking tray and bake for 20 minutes, or until golden.

Place the bacon on a separate tray and bake for 3–5 minutes, or until crisp. Remove the bread from the oven and use one garlic clove, cut in half, to rub the bread slices. Break the bacon into pieces and leave to cool.

Remove the outer leaves of the lettuce. Rinse the inner leaves well, drain, dry and place in a large bowl with the spinach. Add the bacon, croutons, and pine nuts.

Place the remaining oil in a frying pan and heat gently. Add the shallot and cook until they soften, then crush the remaining garlic clove and add to the pan. Whisk in the mustard and vinegar, then gently whisk in the chopped Brie until it has melted. Remove the dressing from the heat and, while it is still warm, pour over the salad and toss gently.

SERVES 4

Artichoke, prosciutto, and arugula salad

4 artichokes
2 eggs, lightly beaten
3 tablespoons fresh
   breadcrumbs
3 tablespoons grated parmesan
   cheese

olive oil, for frying
8 slices prosciutto
3 teaspoons white wine vinegar
1 garlic clove, crushed
3 handfuls arugula, long stalks
   trimmed

Bring a large saucepan of water to a boil. Remove the hard, outer leaves of each artichoke, trim the stem and cut 1 inch off the top. Cut into quarters and remove the furry 'choke'. Boil the pieces for 2 minutes, then drain.

Whisk the eggs in a bowl and mix the seasoned breadcrumbs and parmesan in another bowl. Dip each artichoke quarter into the egg, then roll in the crumb mixture to coat. Fill a frying pan with olive oil to a depth of ¾ inch and heat over medium–high heat. Add the artichokes in batches and fry for 2–3 minutes, or until golden. Remove from the pan and drain on paper towel.

Heat 1 tablespoon of olive oil in a non-stick frying pan over medium–high heat. Cook the prosciutto in two batches for 2 minutes, or until crisp and golden. Remove from the pan, reserving the oil.

Combine the reserved oil, vinegar and garlic with a little salt and pepper. Place the arugula in a bowl, add half of the salad dressing and toss well. Divide the arugula, artichokes, and prosciutto among four plates, and drizzle with the remaining dressing. Sprinkle with sea salt.

SERVES 4

Watercress, feta, and watermelon salad

2 tablespoons sunflower seeds
2 lbs watermelon, cut into ¾-inch cubes
6 oz feta cheese, cut into ¾-inch cubes
2½ cups watercress
2 tablespoons olive oil
1 tablespoon lemon juice
2 teaspoons chopped oregano

Heat a small frying pan over high heat. Add the sunflower seeds and, shaking the pan continuously, dry-fry for 2 minutes, or until toasted and lightly golden.

Put the watermelon, feta, and watercress in a large serving dish and toss gently to combine.

Combine the olive oil, lemon juice, and oregano in a small cup and season to taste. Pour the dressing over the salad and toss together well. Scatter with the toasted sunflower seeds and serve.

SERVES 4

Mushroom and goat's cheese salad

Dressing
2 tablespoons lemon juice
3 tablespoons olive oil
1 teaspoon grated lemon zest

8 large cap mushrooms, stems removed
1 tablespoon chopped thyme

4 garlic cloves, finely chopped
2 tablespoons olive oil
1 cup baby arugula
3½ oz goat's cheese
2 tablespoons chopped Italian parsley

Preheat the oven to 400°F. To make the dressing, combine the juice, oil, and lemon zest in a small bowl.

Put the mushrooms on a large baking tray, sprinkle with the thyme and garlic, then drizzle with the oil. Cover with foil and roast for 20 minutes. Remove the mushrooms from the oven and toss to combine the flavors. Re-cover and roast for a further 10 minutes, or until cooked. Remove the mushrooms from the oven and cut in half.

Place the arugula on a serving platter, top with the mushrooms and crumble the goat's cheese over the top.

Whisk the dressing to ensure it is well combined and drizzle over the salad. Serve sprinkled with the parsley.

SERVES 4–6

Haloumi and asparagus salad with salsa verde

8 oz haloumi cheese
25 small, thin, fresh asparagus spears
2 tablespoons garlic oil
1 small handful basil
1 small handful mint
1 handful Italian parsley
2 tablespoons baby capers, rinsed and squeezed dry
1 garlic clove
2 tablespoons olive oil
1 tablespoon lemon juice
1 tablespoon lime juice
2 handfuls mixed salad leaves (mesclun)

Heat a chargrill pan or barbecue hotplate over medium heat. Cut the haloumi into ½-inch thick slices and cut each slice in half diagonally to make two small triangles. Brush the haloumi and asparagus with the garlic oil. Sear the asparagus for 1 minute or until just tender, and the haloumi until grill marks appear and it is warmed through. Keep warm.

To make the salsa verde, place the herbs, capers, garlic, and oil in a food processor and blend until smooth. Add the citrus juices, and pulse briefly.

Divide the salad leaves among four serving plates. Top with the haloumi and asparagus, and drizzle with a little salsa verde.

SERVES 4

Chicken Waldorf salad

3 cups chicken stock
2 boneless, skinless chicken breasts, skin removed
2 red apples
2 green apples
2 celery stalks, sliced
1 cup toasted walnuts
½ cup mayonnaise
3 tablespoons sour cream
½ teaspoon chopped tarragon
1 baby romaine lettuce

Bring the stock to a boil in a medium saucepan. Remove from the heat, add the chicken to the stock, then cover and allow to cool in the liquid for 10 minutes, by which time the chicken should be cooked.

Cut the apples into bite-sized pieces. Shred the chicken breasts and place in a large bowl with the apple, celery, walnuts, mayonnaise, sour cream, and tarragon. Season and toss well to combine. Separate the lettuce leaves and arrange in a serving bowl. Pile the Waldorf salad over the lettuce and serve.

SERVES 4

Sun-dried tomato and baby spinach salad

2 quarters of preserved lemon
3 cups baby spinach leaves
1⅓ cups sun-dried tomatoes, sliced
8 oz marinated artichoke hearts, drained and chopped
½ cup small black olives
2 tablespoons lemon juice
3 tablespoons olive oil
1 large garlic clove, crushed

Remove and discard the pith and flesh from the preserved lemon. Wash the zest and thinly slice.

Put the spinach leaves in a bowl with the tomato, artichoke, olives, and the preserved lemon slices.

Put the lemon juice, oil, and garlic in a bowl, season and mix well. Pour over the spinach mixture and toss to coat. Serve immediately.

SERVES 6

Chargrilled haloumi
and roast vegetable salad

4 slender eggplants, halved lengthways
1 red pepper, halved and thickly sliced
4 small zucchini, cut in half and halved lengthways
4 tablespoons olive oil
2 garlic cloves, crushed
7 oz haloumi cheese, cut into ¼-inch thick slices
3 cups baby spinach leaves
1 tablespoon balsamic vinegar

Preheat the oven to 425°F. Put the vegetables in a large bowl, add 3 tablespoons of the olive oil and the garlic, season, and toss well to combine.

Put the vegetables in an ovenproof dish in a single layer. Roast for 20–30 minutes, or until tender and browned around the edges.

Meanwhile, lightly brush a chargrill or heavy-based frying pan with oil and cook the haloumi slices for 1–2 minutes each side.

Place the spinach leaves on four serving plates. Top with the roast vegetables and haloumi. Place the remaining oil in a small bowl, add the vinegar and whisk to combine, then pour over the vegetables and haloumi. Serve immediately, warm or at room temperature.

SERVES 4

NOTE: You can use any roasted vegetable, such as sweet potatoes, leeks, and firm, ripe plum tomatoes.

Scallops, ginger, and spinach salad

10½ oz scallops
2 cups baby spinach leaves
1 small red pepper, cut into very fine strips
½ cup bean sprouts, trimmed
1 fl oz sake
1 tablespoon lime juice
2 teaspoons shaved palm sugar or brown sugar
1 teaspoon fish sauce

Lightly brush a chargrill pan or barbecue hotplate with oil. Cook the scallops in batches for 1 minute each side, or until cooked.

Divide the spinach, pepper, and bean sprouts among four plates. Arrange the scallops over the top.

To make the dressing, place the sake, lime juice, palm sugar, and fish sauce in a small bowl and mix together well. Pour over the salad and serve immediately.

SERVES 4

Shrimp and fennel salad

2 lbs 12 oz raw large shrimp,
   peeled and deveined
1 large fennel bulb (about 14 oz), thinly sliced
10½ oz watercress
2 tablespoons finely chopped chives
½ cup extra virgin olive oil
3 tablespoons lemon juice
1 tablespoon dijon mustard
1 large garlic clove, finely chopped

Bring a saucepan of water to a boil. Add the shrimp and simmer for 2 minutes, or until they are pink and cooked through. Drain and leave to cool. Pat the shrimp dry with paper towel and slice in half lengthways. Place in a large bowl.

Add the fennel, watercress, and chives to the bowl and mix well.

To make the dressing, whisk the oil, lemon juice, mustard, and garlic together until combined. Pour the dressing over the salad, season and toss gently. Arrange the salad on serving plates and serve immediately.

SERVES 4

Scallop salad with saffron dressing

pinch of saffron threads
3 tablespoons mayonnaise
1½ tablespoons light whipping cream
1 teaspoon lemon juice
20 scallops
1 oz butter
1 tablespoon olive oil
3 handfuls mixed salad leaves (mesclun)
1 small handful chervil leaves

To make the dressing, place the saffron threads in a bowl and soak in 2 teaspoons of hot water for 10 minutes. Add the mayonnaise and mix well. Stir in the cream, then the lemon juice. Refrigerate until needed.

Heat the butter and oil in a large frying pan over high heat and sear the scallops in small batches for 1 minute on each side.

Divide the mixed salad leaves and chervil among four serving plates, then top each with five scallops. Drizzle the dressing over the scallops and the salad leaves before serving.

SERVES 4

Octopus salad

1 lb 7 oz baby octopus, cleaned
4 oz mixed salad leaves (mesclun)
lemon wedges, to serve

Dressing
2 tablespoons lemon juice
3½ fl oz olive oil
1 garlic clove, thinly sliced
1 tablespoon chopped mint
1 tablespoon chopped Italian parsley
1 teaspoon dijon mustard
pinch of cayenne pepper

Bring a large saucepan of water to a boil and add the octopus. Simmer for about 8–10 minutes, or until the octopus is tender to the point of a knife.

Meanwhile, make a dressing by mixing together the lemon juice, olive oil, garlic, mint, parsley, mustard, and cayenne pepper. Season to taste.

Drain the octopus well and put in a bowl. Pour the dressing over the top and cool for a few minutes before refrigerating. Chill for at least 3 hours before serving on a bed of salad leaves. Drizzle a little of the dressing over the top and serve with lemon wedges.

SERVES 4

Squid salad

Dressing

2 large garlic cloves, crushed

2 teaspoons grated fresh ginger

3 small fresh red chilies, seeded
  and thinly sliced

2 tablespoons grated palm
  sugar or brown sugar

2 tablespoons fish sauce

2 tablespoons lime juice

½ teaspoon sesame oil

1 lb 2 oz squid tubes, cleaned

6 kaffir lime leaves

1 lemon grass stem, white part
  only, chopped

3–4 shallots, thinly sliced

1 small cucumber, cut in half
  lengthways and thinly sliced

3 tablespoons chopped cilantro
  leaves

1 small handful mint leaves

5½ oz oakleaf or coral lettuce,
  leaves separated

fried shallot flakes,
  to garnish (optional)

To make the dressing, heat the garlic, ginger, chili, palm sugar, fish sauce, lime juice, sesame oil, and 1 tablespoon water in a saucepan over low heat.

Cut the squid in half lengthways. Clean and remove any quills. Score a criss-cross pattern on the inside of the squid. Cut the squid into 1¼-inch pieces.

Place the kaffir lime leaves, lemon grass and 5 cups water in a saucepan and bring to a boil. Reduce the heat and simmer for 5 minutes. Add half the squid pieces and cook for 30 seconds, or until they begin to curl up. Remove and keep warm. Repeat with the remaining squid. Discard the lime leaves, lemon grass, and liquid.

Put the squid, shallots, cucumber, cilantro, mint, lettuce, and dressing in a large bowl and toss together. Serve garnished with the shallot flakes, if using.

SERVES 4

Crab salad with mango and coconut

2 garlic cloves, peeled
2 small red chilies
2 tablespoons dried shrimp
2 tablespoons fish sauce
3 tablespoons lime juice
3 teaspoons palm sugar or
   brown sugar
½ cup shredded coconut
1½ cups shredded green mango
1 small handful mint leaves
   (torn, if very big)
1 small handful cilantro leaves
3 kaffir lime leaves, shredded

2 teaspoons thinly shredded
   pickled ginger
1 lb 2 oz fresh crabmeat

banana leaves, crushed toasted
   peanuts, and lime wedges,
   to serve (optional)

Preheat the oven to 350°F. Put the garlic, chilies, dried shrimp, and ½ teaspoon salt in a mortar and pestle. Pound to a paste, then whisk in the fish sauce, lime juice, and palm sugar with a fork.

Put the shredded coconut on a baking tray and bake for 3–5 minutes, shaking the tray occasionally to ensure even toasting. Watch the coconut closely, as it will burn easily.

Put the shredded mango in a large bowl and add the mint, cilantro, kaffir lime leaves, ginger, coconut, and crabmeat. Pour on the dressing and toss together gently.

Place a piece of banana leaf (if using) in each serving bowl. Top with crab salad, sprinkle with the peanuts and serve immediately with lime wedges.

SERVES 4–6

Somen noodle salad

Sesame dressing
3 tablespoons sesame seeds, toasted
2½ tablespoons shoyu or light soy sauce
2 tablespoons rice vinegar
2 teaspoons sugar
½ teaspoon grated fresh ginger
½ teaspoon dashi granules

4½ oz dried somen noodles
3½ oz snow peas, finely sliced on the diagonal
3½ oz daikon radish, julienned
1 carrot, julienned
1 scallion, sliced on the diagonal
1 cup baby spinach leaves
2 teaspoons toasted sesame seeds

To make the dressing, place the sesame seeds in a mortar and pestle and grind until fine and moist. Combine the soy sauce, rice vinegar, sugar, ginger, dashi granules, and ½ cup water in a saucepan and bring to a boil over high heat. Reduce the heat to medium and simmer, stirring, for 2 minutes, or until the dashi granules have dissolved.

Remove from the heat. Cool. Gradually combine with the ground sesame seeds, stirring to form a thick dressing.

Cook the noodles in a saucepan of boiling water for 2 minutes, or until tender. Drain, rinse under cold water and cool. Cut into 4-inch lengths.

Put the snow peas in a shallow bowl with the daikon, carrot, scallion, spinach leaves, and the noodles. Add the dressing and toss. Refrigerate until ready to serve. Just before serving, sprinkle the top with the toasted sesame seeds.

SERVES 4

Vietnamese
shrimp salad

1 small Chinese cabbage, finely shredded
3 tablespoons sugar
3 tablespoons fish sauce
4 tablespoons lime juice
1 tablespoon white vinegar
1 small red onion, finely sliced
1 lb 10 oz cooked jumbo shrimps,
   peeled and deveined, with tails intact
1 small handful cilantro leaves, chopped
1 small handful Vietnamese mint leaves, chopped (see Note)

Put the Chinese cabbage in a large bowl, cover with cling wrap and chill for 30 minutes.

Put the sugar, fish sauce, lime juice, vinegar, and ½ teaspoon salt in a small bowl and mix well.

Toss together the shredded cabbage, onion, shrimp, cilantro, mint, and dressing, and garnish with the extra mint leaves.

SERVES 6

NOTE: Vietnamese mint is available from Asian markets.

Thai marinated octopus salad

8 baby octopus, cut in half
1 cup sweet chili sauce
2 tablespoons lime juice
1 lemon grass stem, white part only, finely chopped
2 small cucumbers
1¾ oz butter lettuce, torn into rough pieces
1¾ oz cilantro, with stalks

Using a small knife, carefully cut between the head and tentacles of the octopus, just below the eyes. Grasp the body of the octopus and push the beak out with your finger. Cut the eyes from the head of the octopus and discard the eye section. Carefully slit through one side, avoiding the ink sac, and scrape out the gut. Rinse under running water to remove any remaining gut.

Put the octopus in a bowl and add the chili sauce, lime juice, and lemon grass. Stir until well mixed. Cover with cling wrap and chill for 4 hours.

Cut the cucumbers into 2½-inch lengths, scoop out the seeds and discard. Cut the cucumber into batons.

Heat a chargrill pan or barbecue hotplate until hot. Remove the octopus from the marinade, reserving the marinade, and cook for 3 minutes, or until cooked through. Cool slightly. Arrange the lettuce and cilantro around the edge of a plate, and pile the octopus in the center.

Add the remaining marinade to the chargrill pan and heat for 2 minutes. Toss the cucumber through the marinade to warm, then spoon over the salad.

SERVES 4

Roasted fennel
and orange salad

8 baby fennel bulbs
3½ fl oz olive oil
2 oranges
1 tablespoon lemon juice
1 red onion, halved and thinly
    sliced

3½ oz Kalamata olives
2 tablespoons roughly chopped
    mint
1 tablespoon roughly chopped
    Italian parsley

Preheat the oven to 400°F. Trim the fronds from the fennel and reserve. Remove the stalks and cut a slice off the base of each fennel ¼-inch thick. Slice each fennel into 6 wedges, put in a baking dish and drizzle with 3 tablespoons olive oil. Season well. Bake for 40–45 minutes, or until tender and slightly caramelized. Turn once or twice during cooking. Allow to cool.

Cut a thin slice off the top and bottom of each orange. Using a sharp knife, slice off the skin and pith. Remove as much pith as possible. Slice down the side of a segment between the flesh and the membrane. Repeat with the other side and lift the segment out. Do this over a bowl to catch the juices. Repeat with all the segments on both oranges. Squeeze out any juice remaining in the membranes.

Whisk the remaining oil into the orange and lemon juice until emulsified. Season well. Combine the orange segments, onion, and olives in a bowl, pour on half the dressing and add half the mint. Mix well. Transfer to a serving dish. Top with the fennel, drizzle with the remaining dressing, and scatter the parsley and remaining mint over the top. Chop the reserved fronds and sprinkle over the salad.

SERVES 4

mains

Thai beef salad

4 tablespoons lime juice
2 tablespoons fish sauce
2 teaspoons grated palm sugar or brown sugar
1 garlic clove, crushed
1 tablespoon finely chopped cilantro roots and stems
1 lemon grass stem, white part only, finely chopped
2 small red chilies, finely sliced
2 x 7 oz boneless beef sirloin steaks
5½ oz mixed salad leaves (mesclun)
½ red onion, cut into thin wedges
1 handful cilantro leaves
1 small handful mint leaves, torn
9 oz cherry tomatoes, halved
1 cucumber, halved lengthways and
   thinly sliced on the diagonal

Mix together the lime juice, fish sauce, palm sugar, garlic, chopped cilantro, lemon grass, and chili until the sugar has dissolved.

Preheat the chargrill pan or barbecue hotplate to medium–high direct heat and cook the steaks for 4 minutes on each side, or until medium. Let the steaks cool, then slice thinly across the grain.

Put the salad leaves, onion, cilantro leaves, mint, tomatoes, and cucumber in a large bowl, add the beef and dressing, toss together and serve immediately.

SERVES 4

Chicken and spinach salad with sesame dressing

1 lb baby spinach leaves
1 cucumber, peeled and diced
4 scallions, shredded
2 carrots, cut into matchsticks
2 boneless, skinless chicken breasts, cooked
2 tablespoons tahini
2 tablespoons lime juice
3 teaspoons sesame oil
1 teaspoon sugar
pinch of chili flakes
2 tablespoons sesame seeds
1 large handful cilantro leaves

Put the spinach in a large bowl. Scatter the cucumber, scallion, and carrot over the top. Shred the chicken breast into long pieces and scatter it over the vegetables.

Mix together the tahini, lime juice, sesame oil, sugar, and chili flakes, then add salt to taste. Drizzle over the salad.

Put the sesame seeds in a frying pan over low heat and dry-fry for 1–2 minutes, stirring, or until starting to brown. Add to the salad. Scatter the cilantro leaves over the top. Toss just before serving.

SERVES 4

Tuna and white bean salad

2 tuna steaks
1 small red onion, thinly sliced
1 firm, ripe tomato, seeded and
    chopped
1 small red pepper, thinly sliced
1 lb 12 oz canned cannellini
    beans
2 garlic cloves, crushed
1 teaspoon chopped thyme

4 tablespoons finely chopped
    Italian parsley
1½ tablespoons lemon juice
4 tablespoons extra virgin olive
    oil
1 teaspoon honey
olive oil, for brushing
2¼ cups arugula
1 teaspoon lemon zest

Put the tuna steaks on a plate, sprinkle with cracked black pepper on both sides, cover with cling wrap and refrigerate until needed.

Combine the onion, tomato, and pepper in a large bowl. Rinse the cannellini beans under cold running water for 30 seconds, drain and add to the bowl with the garlic, thyme, and 3 tablespoons of the parsley.

Put the lemon juice, oil, and honey in a small saucepan, bring to a boil, then simmer, stirring, for 1 minute, or until the honey dissolves. Remove from the heat.

Brush a chargrill pan or barbecue hotplate with olive oil, and heat until very hot. Cook the tuna for 1 minute on each side. The meat should still be pink in the middle. Slice into 1¼-inch cubes and combine with the salad. Pour on the warm dressing and toss well.

Place the arugula on a platter. Top with the salad, season and garnish with the lemon zest and remaining parsley.

SERVES 4–6

Greek pepper lamb salad

10½ oz boneless double lamb loin chops
1½ tablespoons cracked black pepper
3 vine-ripened tomatoes, cut into 8 wedges
2 cucumbers, sliced
5½ oz lemon and garlic marinated Kalamata
    olives, drained (reserving 1½ tablespoons oil)
⅔ cup cubed feta cheese
¾ teaspoon dried oregano
1 tablespoon lemon juice
1 tablespoon extra virgin olive oil

Roll the loin chops in the pepper, pressing the pepper on with your fingers. Cover and refrigerate for about 15 minutes. Place the tomato, cucumber, olives, feta, and ½ teaspoon of the dried oregano in a bowl.

Heat a chargrill pan or barbecue hotplate, brush with oil and when very hot, cook the lamb for 2–3 minutes on each side, or until cooked to your liking. Keep warm.

Whisk the lemon juice, extra virgin olive oil, reserved Kalamata oil, and the remaining dried oregano together well. Season. Pour half the dressing over the salad, toss together and arrange on a serving platter.

Cut the lamb on the diagonal into ½-inch thick slices and arrange on top of the salad. Pour the rest of the dressing on top and serve.

SERVES 4

Chicken Caesar salad

Caesar dressing
1 egg yolk
1 garlic clove, crushed
3 anchovy fillets
1 teaspoon dijon mustard
½ cup oil
1 tablespoon lemon juice
½ teaspoon worcestershire sauce

1 tablespoon grated parmesan
   cheese
4 boneless, skinless chicken
   thighs
4 tablespoons olive oil
12 x ½-inch thick slices baguette
1 garlic clove, halved
4 bacon slices
2 baby romaine lettuces

Put the egg yolk, garlic, anchovies, and mustard in a food processor and process. With the motor running, add the oil in a thin stream and process until the mixture is thick. Stir in the lemon juice, worcestershire sauce, and parmesan. Season.

Put the chicken thighs in a bowl with 1 tablespoon of the olive oil, season to taste and turn to coat well in the oil.

Preheat a chargrill pan or babecue hotplate to medium–high heat. Brush the baguette slices with the remaining olive oil, and toast for 1 minute on each side. Rub both sides of each piece of toast with the cut clove of garlic and keep warm.

Cook the chicken on the chargrill pan for 5 minutes on each side, or until cooked through. Cut into ½-inch thick strips. Cook the bacon for 3 minutes each side, or until crisp, then break it into ¾-inch pieces.

Tear the romaine leaves into bite-sized pieces and toss in a large bowl with the dressing, bacon, and chicken. Serve with the garlic croutons.

SERVES 4–6

Squid salad with salsa verde

1 lb 12 oz squid, scored and
    sliced into 1½-inch diamonds
2 tablespoons olive oil
2 tablespoons lime juice
5½ oz green beans
5½ oz thin, fresh asparagus
    spears
1 teaspoon olive oil, extra
2 cups baby arugula

Salsa verde
1 thick slice white bread, crusts
    removed
5 fl oz olive oil
3 tablespoons finely chopped
    Italian parsley
2 teaspoons grated lemon zest
3 tablespoons lemon juice
2 anchovy fillets, finely chopped
2 tablespoons capers, drained
1 garlic clove, crushed

Combine the squid pieces with the olive oil, lime juice, and season. Cover with cling wrap and refrigerate for 2 hours.

To make the salsa verde, break the bread into chunks and drizzle with 2 tablespoons of the oil. Put the bread and remaining oil in a food processor with the remaining salsa ingredients, and blend to a paste.

Trim the green beans and asparagus, and cut in half on the diagonal. Blanch the beans for 3 minutes, refresh under cold water, then drain. Blanch the asparagus for 1–2 minutes, refresh in cold water, then drain.

Heat the extra oil in a frying pan over high heat, and cook the marinated squid in batches for 3 minutes per batch, or until cooked. Cool slightly. Combine the green beans, asparagus, arugula, and squid. Add 3 tablespoons of the salsa verde and toss. Arrange on a serving platter and drizzle with another tablespoon of salsa verde.

SERVES 4

Spicy lamb and noodle salad

1 tablespoon Chinese five-spice
3 tablespoons vegetable oil
2 garlic cloves, crushed
2 boneless double lamb loin
  chops (about 9 oz each)
1 lb 2 oz fresh Shanghai (wheat)
  noodles
1½ teaspoons sesame oil
2¾ oz snow pea sprouts
½ red pepper, thinly sliced
4 scallions, thinly sliced on the
  diagonal

2 tablespoons sesame seeds,
  toasted

Dressing
1 tablespoon finely chopped
  fresh ginger
1 tablespoon Chinese black
  vinegar
1 tablespoon Chinese rice wine
2 tablespoons peanut oil
2 teaspoons chili oil

Combine the five-spice, 2 tablespoons of the vegetable oil, and garlic in a large bowl. Add the lamb and turn to coat well. Cover and marinate for 30 minutes.

Cook the noodles in a saucepan of boiling water for 4–5 minutes, or until tender. Drain, rinse under cold water and drain again. Add the sesame oil and toss.

Heat the remaining vegetable oil in a frying pan. Cook the lamb over medium–high heat for 3 minutes each side for medium–rare. Rest for 5 minutes, then thinly slice across the grain.

To make the dressing, combine the ginger, Chinese black vinegar, rice wine, peanut oil, and chili oil.

Put the noodles, lamb strips, snow pea sprouts, pepper, scallions, and the dressing in a bowl and toss gently. Sprinkle with the sesame seeds.

SERVES 4

Asian pork salad

2 teaspoons rice vinegar
1 small red chili, finely chopped
2 tablespoons light soy sauce
1 teaspoon julienned fresh ginger
¼ teaspoon sesame oil
1 star anise
2 teaspoons lime juice
9 oz Chinese barbecued pork (char siu) (see Note)
3½ oz snow pea sprouts
2 scallions, thinly sliced on the diagonal
½ red pepper, thinly sliced

To make the dressing, combine the vinegar, chili, soy sauce, ginger, sesame oil, star anise, and lime juice in a small saucepan. Gently warm for 2 minutes, or until just about to come to the boil, then set aside to cool. Once cool, remove the star anise.

Thinly slice the pork and put in a serving bowl. Pick over the sprouts, discarding any brown or broken ones, and add to the pork. Add the scallions and pepper, pour over the dressing and toss well.

SERVES 4

NOTE: Chinese barbecued pork (*char siu*) is a traditional means of roasting pork. The meat is first seasoned with a number of spices and flavorings which give the meat its characteristic shiny red glaze. You can buy *char siu* from Chinese restaurants and Asian food stores.

Roasted tomato
and pasta salad with pesto

5 fl oz olive oil
1 lb 2 oz cherry tomatoes
5 garlic cloves, unpeeled
14 oz penne
4 tablespoons pesto
3 tablespoons balsamic vinegar
basil leaves, to garnish

Preheat the oven to 350°F. Put 2 tablespoons of the oil in a roasting dish and place in the oven for 5 minutes. Add the tomatoes and garlic to the dish, season and toss until well coated. Return to the oven and roast for 30 minutes.

Meanwhile, cook the pasta in a large saucepan of boiling salted water until *al dente*. Drain and transfer to a large serving bowl.

Squeeze the flesh from the roasted garlic cloves into a bowl. Add the remaining oil, the pesto, vinegar, and 3 tablespoons of the tomato cooking juices. Season and toss to combine. Add to the pasta and mix well, ensuring that the pasta is coated in the dressing. Gently stir in the cherry tomatoes, then scatter with basil. Serve warm or cold.

SERVES 4

Asian tofu salad

1 large red pepper
1 large green pepper
6 oz bean sprouts
4 scallions, sliced on the diagonal
1 small handful cilantro leaves, chopped
1 lb Chinese cabbage, shredded
3 tablespoons chopped roasted peanuts
1 lb firm tofu
3 tablespoons peanut oil

Dressing
2 tablespoons sweet chili sauce
2 tablespoons lime juice
½ teaspoon sesame oil
1½ tablespoons light soy sauce
1 garlic clove, finely chopped
3 teaspoons finely grated fresh ginger
3 tablespoons peanut oil

Thinly slice the peppers, and combine with the bean sprouts, scallion, cilantro, cabbage, and peanuts.

Drain the liquid from the tofu and cut into 3- x ¾-inch thick slices. Heat the oil in a large frying pan. Cook the tofu for 2–3 minutes on each side, or until it is golden with a crispy edge, and add to the salad.

To make the dressing, mix together the chili sauce, lime juice, sesame oil, soy, garlic, and ginger. Whisk in the peanut oil, then toss through the salad and serve immediately.

SERVES 4

Indian marinated chicken salad

3 tablespoons lemon juice
1½ teaspoons garam masala
1 teaspoon ground turmeric
1 tablespoon finely grated fresh
  ginger
2 garlic cloves, finely chopped
3½ tablespoons vegetable oil
3 boneless, skinless chicken
  breasts
1 onion, thinly sliced
2 zucchini, thinly sliced on the
  diagonal

3½ oz watercress
1 cup peas
2 firm, ripe tomatoes, finely
  chopped
1 handful cilantro leaves

Dressing
1 teaspoon cumin seeds
½ teaspoon coriander seeds
4 tablespoons plain yogurt
2 tablespoons chopped mint
2 tablespoons lemon juice

Combine the lemon juice, garam masala, turmeric, ginger, garlic, and 2 teaspoons of the oil in a bowl. Add the chicken and onion. Toss. Cover, and refrigerate for 1 hour.

Remove and discard the onion, then heat 2 tablespoons of the oil in a frying pan. Cook the chicken for about 4–5 minutes on each side, or until cooked through. Cut each breast across the grain into ½-inch thick slices.

Heat the remaining oil in the pan and cook the zucchini for 2 minutes, or until lightly golden. Toss with the watercress in a large bowl. Cook the peas in boiling water for 5 minutes, or until tender, then drain. Rinse under cold water to cool. Add to the salad with the tomato, chicken, and cilantro.

To make the dressing, roast the cumin and coriander seeds in a dry frying pan for 1–2 minutes, or until fragrant. Remove, then pound the seeds to a powder. Mix with the yogurt, mint, and lemon juice, then fold through the salad.

SERVES 4

Fusilli salad with sherry vinaigrette

10½ oz fusilli
9 oz cauliflower florets
½ cup olive oil
16 slices pancetta
1 large handful small sage
    leaves
⅔ cup pine nuts, toasted
2 tablespoons finely chopped
    shallots

1½ tablespoons sherry vinegar
1 small red chili, finely chopped
2 garlic cloves, crushed
1 teaspoon brown sugar
2 tablespoons orange juice
1 handful Italian parsley, finely
    chopped
4 tablespoons shaved parmesan
    cheese

Cook the fusilli in a large saucepan of rapidly boiling salted water for 12 minutes, or until *al dente*. Drain and refresh under cold water until it is cool. Drain well. Blanch the cauliflower florets in boiling water for 3 minutes, then drain and cool.

Heat 1 tablespoon of the olive oil in a non-stick frying pan and cook the pancetta for 2 minutes, or until crisp. Drain on crumpled paper towel.

Add 1 tablespoon of oil and cook the sage leaves for 1 minute, or until crisp. Drain on paper towel. In a bowl, combine the pasta, pine nuts, and cauliflower.

Heat the remaining olive oil, add the shallots and cook for 2 minutes, or until soft. Remove from the heat then add the vinegar, chili, garlic, brown sugar, orange juice, and parsley. Pour the warm dressing over the pasta and toss to combine.

Place the salad in a serving bowl. Crumble the pancetta over the top and scatter with sage leaves and shaved parmesan. Serve warm.

SERVES 6

Marinated grilled tofu salad

4 tablespoons tamari, shoyu, or
  light soy sauce
2 teaspoons oil
2 garlic cloves, crushed
1 teaspoon grated fresh ginger
1 teaspoon chili paste
1 lb 2 oz firm tofu, cut into
  ¾-inch cubes
14 oz mixed salad leaves
  (mesclun)
1 cucumber, finely sliced

9 oz cherry tomatoes, halved
2 teaspoons oil, extra

Dressing
2 teaspoons white miso paste
  (see Note)
2 tablespoons mirin
1 teaspoon sesame oil
1 teaspoon grated fresh ginger
1 teaspoon finely chopped chives
1 tablespoon toasted sesame
  seeds

Mix together the tamari, oil, garlic, ginger, chili paste, and ½ teaspoon salt. Add the tofu and mix. Marinate for at least 10 minutes. Drain and reserve the marinade.

To make the dressing, combine the miso with ½ cup hot water and leave until the miso dissolves. Add the mirin, sesame oil, ginger, chives, and sesame seeds and stir thoroughly until it begins to thicken.

Combine the mixed salad leaves, cucumber, and tomato in a serving bowl.

Heat the extra oil in a chargrill pan or barbecue hotplate. Add the tofu and cook over medium heat for 4 minutes, or until golden brown. Pour on the reserved marinade and cook for 1 minute over high heat. Remove from the pan and allow to cool for 5 minutes. Add the tofu to the salad, drizzle with the dressing and toss well.

SERVES 4

NOTE: Miso, made from fermented soybean, is available from Japanese food stores.

Beef satay salad

2 teaspoons tamarind pulp
½ teaspoon sesame oil
2 tablespoons soy sauce
2 teaspoons brown sugar
2 garlic cloves, crushed
1 tablespoon lime juice
1 lb 9 oz rump steak
2 red chilies, chopped
½ teaspoon shrimp paste
1 garlic clove
6 shallots
2 teaspoons peanut oil
1 cup coconut milk
1 tablespoon lime juice

¾ cup unsalted roasted
   peanuts, finely ground in a
   food processor
1 tablespoon kecap manis
1 tablespoon brown sugar
1 tablespoon fish sauce
2 kaffir lime leaves, shredded
1 tablespoon peanut oil
6 romaine lettuce leaves
1 red pepper
6½ oz bean sprouts
2 tablespoons fried onion flakes

Combine the tamarind pulp and 3 tablespoons boiling water and allow to cool. Mash the pulp to dissolve it, then strain, reserving the liquid. Discard the pulp.

Combine the sesame oil, soy sauce, sugar, garlic, lime juice, and 2 tablespoons of the tamarind water. Add the steak and cover with cling wrap. Chill for 2 hours.

Process the chilies, shrimp paste, garlic, and shallots to a paste in a food processor. Heat the oil in a frying pan and cook the paste for 3 minutes. Add the coconut milk, lime juice, peanuts, remaining tamarind water, kecap manis, sugar, fish sauce, and kaffir lime leaves. Cook until thickened. Thin with ½ cup water and return to a boil for 2 minutes. Season. Heat the peanut oil in a frying pan over high heat, and cook the steak for 3 minutes on each side. Slice. Toss the steak slices in a bowl with shredded lettuce, pepper, and the bean sprouts. Drizzle with the sauce and sprinkle with the onion flakes.

SERVES 4

Warm pasta and sweet potato salad

1 lb 10 oz sweet potato
2 tablespoons extra virgin olive oil
1 lb 2 oz casarecci pasta
11½ oz marinated feta cheese in oil
3 tablespoons balsamic vinegar
5½ oz thin, fresh asparagus spears, cut into short lengths
2 cups baby arugula or baby spinach leaves
2 firm vine-ripened tomatoes, chopped
3 tablespoons pine nuts, toasted

Preheat the oven to 400°F. Peel the sweet potato and cut into large pieces. Put in a baking dish, drizzle with the olive oil and season. Bake for 20 minutes, or until the sweet potato is tender.

Cook the pasta in a large saucepan of boiling salted water until *al dente*. Drain well.

Drain the oil from the feta and whisk 3 tablespoons of the oil together with the balsamic vinegar to make a dressing.

Steam the asparagus until bright green and tender. Drain well.

Combine the pasta, sweet potato, asparagus, arugula, feta, tomatoes, and pine nuts in a bowl. Add the dressing and toss gently. Season and serve immediately.

SERVES 4

Pepper-crusted
salmon salad

- 1 tablespoon coarsely ground black pepper
- 4 salmon steaks, skin removed
- 4 tablespoons mayonnaise
- 1½ tablespoons lemon juice
- 2 teaspoons creamed horseradish
- 1 small garlic clove, crushed
- 2 tablespoons chopped Italian parsley
- 3½ oz watercress
- 3 tablespoons olive oil
- 1 oz butter
- 3½ oz butter lettuce

Mix the pepper and ¼ teaspoon salt together in a bowl. Coat both sides of each salmon steak, pressing the pepper down firmly with your fingers. Chill for 30 minutes.

Blend the mayonnaise, lemon juice, horseradish, garlic, parsley, 2¼ oz of the watercress, 1 tablespoon of the oil, and 1 tablespoon of warm water in a food processor for 1 minute. Chill.

Heat the butter and 1 tablespoon of the oil in a large frying pan until bubbling. Add the salmon and cook over medium–high heat for 2–3 minutes each side, or until cooked to your liking. Remove from the pan and allow to cool slightly.

Wash and dry the butter lettuce, and tear into small pieces. Arrange the lettuce and remaining watercress in the center of four serving plates, and drizzle lightly with the remaining olive oil. Break each salmon steak into four or five pieces and arrange over the lettuce. Pour the dressing over the salmon and in a circle around the outside of the leaves.

SERVES 4

Shrimp, mango, and macadamia salad

1 radicchio heart
1 large handful basil leaves, torn
1 cup watercress
24 cooked jumbo shrimp, peeled and
    deveined with tails intact
3 tablespoons macadamia oil
3 tablespoons extra virgin olive oil
1 cup macadamia nuts, coarsely chopped
2 garlic cloves, crushed
3 tablespoons lemon juice
1 ripe mango, cut into small dice

Remove the outer green leaves from the radicchio, leaving only the tender pink leaves. Tear any large leaves in half and arrange in a shallow serving bowl. Scatter with half of the basil leaves and the watercress, and toss lightly. Arrange the shrimp over the salad leaves.

Heat the oils in a small frying pan over medium heat. Add the nuts and cook for 5 minutes, or until golden. Add the garlic and cook for a further 30 seconds, then remove from the heat and add the lemon juice and mango. Season to taste, pour over the salad and scatter with the remaining basil leaves.

SERVES 4

Warm chicken and pasta salad

13 oz penne
3½ fl oz olive oil
4 long, thin eggplants, thinly
    sliced on the diagonal
2 boneless, skinless chicken
    breasts
2 teaspoons lemon juice
½ cup chopped Italian parsley
10 oz chargrilled red pepper,
    drained and sliced

7 thin, fresh asparagus spears,
    trimmed, blanched and cut
    into 2-inch lengths
½ cup finely sliced sun-dried
    tomatoes
grated parmesan cheese,
    (optional)

Cook the pasta in a large saucepan of boiling salted water until *al dente*. Drain, return to the pan and keep warm.

Heat 2 tablespoons of the oil in a large frying pan over high heat and cook the eggplant for 4–5 minutes, or until golden and cooked through.

Heat a lightly oiled chargrill pan or barbecue hotplate over high heat and cook the chicken for 5 minutes on each side, or until browned and fully cooked. Cut into thick slices.

Combine the lemon juice, parsley, and the remaining oil in a small jar and shake well. Return the pasta to the heat, toss through the dressing, chicken, eggplant, pepper, asparagus, and tomato until well mixed and warmed through. Season with black pepper. Serve warm with grated parmesan, if desired.

SERVES 4

Vietnamese
chicken salad

3 chicken breasts or 6 chicken thighs, cooked
2 tablespoons lime juice
1½ tablespoons fish sauce
¼ teaspoon sugar
1–2 bird's eye chilies, finely chopped
1 garlic clove, crushed
2 shallots, finely sliced
2 handfuls bean sprouts
1 large handful shredded Chinese cabbage
4 tablespoons Vietnamese mint or mint leaves, finely chopped

Take the flesh off the chicken bones and shred it. Discard the skin and bones.

Mix together the lime juice, fish sauce, sugar, chili, garlic, and shallot.

Bring a saucepan of water to a boil and add the bean sprouts. After 10 seconds, drain and rinse under cold water to stop them cooking any longer.

Mix the bean sprouts with the Chinese cabbage, mint, and chicken. Pour the dressing over the salad and toss everything together well.

SERVES 4

Seafood salad

1 lb 2 oz small squid
2 lbs 4 oz large clams
2 lbs 4 oz black mussels
1 lb 2 oz raw medium shrimp, peeled
   and deveined, with tails intact
5 tablespoons finely chopped Italian parsley

Dressing
2 tablespoons lemon juice
4 tablespoons olive oil
1 garlic clove, crushed

Gently pull apart the body and tentacles of the squid to separate. Remove the head by cutting below the eyes. Push out the beak and discard. Pull the quill from the body of the squid and discard. Under cold running water, pull away all the skin. Rinse well, then slice the squid into rings.

Scrub the clams and mussels and remove the beards. Rinse under running water. Fill a saucepan with ¾ inch of water, add the clams and mussels, cover, and boil for 4–5 minutes. Remove, reserving the liquid. Discard any that do not open. Remove the mussels and clams from their shells and place in a bowl.

Bring 4 cups water to a boil and add the shrimp and squid. Cook for 3–4 minutes, or until the shrimp turn pink and the squid is tender. Drain and add to the clams and mussels.

To make the dressing, whisk all of the ingredients together. Season. Pour over the seafood, add 4 tablespoons of the parsley and toss to coat. Cover and refrigerate for 30–40 minutes. Sprinkle with the remaining parsley.

SERVES 4

Chili chicken and cashew salad

3 tablespoons sweet chili sauce
2 tablespoons lime juice
2 teaspoons fish sauce
2 tablespoons chopped cilantro leaves
1 garlic clove, crushed
1 small red chili, finely chopped
1½ teaspoons grated fresh ginger
2 tablespoons olive oil
3 boneless, skinless chicken breasts
3½ oz mixed salad leaves (mesclun)
9 oz cherry tomatoes, halved
1 cucumber, cut into bite-sized chunks
1¾ oz snow pea sprouts, trimmed
½ cup cashew nuts, roughly chopped

Combine the chili sauce, lime juice, fish sauce, cilantro, garlic, chili, ginger, and 1 tablespoon of the oil in a large bowl.

Heat the remaining oil in a frying pan or chargrill pan over medium heat until hot, and cook the chicken for 5–8 minutes on each side, or until cooked through. Slice each breast widthways into ½-inch thick slices and toss in the bowl with the dressing. Leave to cool slightly.

Combine the salad leaves, cherry tomato, cucumber chunks, and snow pea sprouts in a serving bowl. Add the chicken and all of the dressing, and toss gently until the leaves are lightly coated. Scatter with chopped cashews and serve.

SERVES 4

Lamb, pepper, and cucumber salad

1 red onion, very thinly sliced
1 red pepper, very thinly sliced
1 green pepper, very thinly sliced
2 large cucumbers, cut into batons
4 tablespoons shredded mint
3 tablespoons chopped dill
3 tablespoons olive oil
1 lb 5 oz boneless double lamb loin chops
4 tablespoons lemon juice
2 small garlic cloves, crushed
3½ fl oz extra virgin olive oil

Combine the onion, red and green pepper, cucumber, mint, and dill in a large bowl.

Heat a chargrill pan or frying pan until hot. Drizzle with the oil and cook the lamb for 2–3 minutes on each side, or until it is tender but still a little pink. Remove from the pan and allow to rest for 5 minutes. Thinly slice the lamb and add to the salad, tossing to mix.

Combine the lemon juice and garlic in a small jug, then whisk in the oil with a fork until well combined. Season, then gently toss the dressing through the salad.

SERVES 4

Warm shrimp, arugula, and feta salad

4 scallions, chopped
4 firm, ripe plum tomatoes, chopped
1 red pepper, chopped
14 oz canned chickpeas, drained
1 tablespoon chopped dill
3 tablespoons finely shredded basil
3 tablespoons extra virgin olive oil
2¼ oz butter
2 lbs 4 oz shrimp, peeled
  and deveined, with tails intact
2 small red chilies, finely chopped
4 garlic cloves, crushed
2 tablespoons lemon juice
10½ oz arugula
5½ oz feta cheese

Put the scallion, tomato, pepper, chickpeas, dill, and shredded basil in a large bowl and toss together well.

Heat the oil and butter in a large frying pan or wok, add the shrimp and cook, stirring, over high heat for 3 minutes. Add the chili and garlic and continue cooking for 2 minutes, or until the shrimp turn pink. Remove the pan from the heat and stir in the lemon juice.

Arrange the arugula leaves on a large serving platter, top with the tomato and chickpea mixture, then the shrimp mixture. Crumble the feta cheese over the top, then serve.

SERVES 4

Ground pork and noodle salad

1 tablespoon peanut oil
1 lb 2 oz ground pork
2 garlic cloves, finely chopped
1 lemon grass stem, white part
  only, finely chopped
2–3 shallots, thinly sliced
3 teaspoons finely grated fresh
  ginger
1 small red chili, finely chopped
5 kaffir lime leaves, very finely
  shredded
6 oz mung bean noodles
1¼ cups baby spinach leaves
1 cup roughly chopped cilantro
  leaves

1 cup peeled, finely chopped
  fresh pineapple
1 small handful mint leaves

Dressing
1½ tablespoons shaved palm
  sugar or brown sugar
2 tablespoons fish sauce
4 tablespoons lime juice
2 teaspoons sesame oil
2 teaspoons peanut oil, extra

Heat a wok until very hot, add the peanut oil and swirl to coat the wok. Add the pork and stir-fry in batches over high heat for 5 minutes, or until lightly golden. Add the garlic, lemon grass, shallot, grated ginger, chili, and kaffir lime leaves, and stir-fry for a further 1–2 minutes, or until fragrant.

Place the noodles in a large bowl and cover with boiling water for 30 seconds, or until softened. Rinse under cold water and drain well. Toss in a bowl with the spinach, cilantro, pineapple, mint, and pork mixture.

To make the dressing, mix together the palm sugar, fish sauce, and lime juice. Add the sesame oil and extra peanut oil, and whisk. Toss through the salad and season.

SERVES 4

Roast duck salad
with chili dressing

½ teaspoon chili flakes
2½ tablespoons fish sauce
1 tablespoon lime juice
2 teaspoons grated palm sugar or brown sugar
1 Chinese roasted duck
1 small red onion, thinly sliced
1 tablespoon julienned fresh ginger
4 tablespoons roughly chopped cilantro leaves
4 tablespoons roughly chopped mint
½ cup roasted cashews
3¼ oz butter lettuce

Put the chili flakes in a frying pan and dry-fry for 30 seconds, then grind to a powder in a mortar and pestle or spice grinder. Combine the chili with the fish sauce, lime juice, and palm sugar in a bowl, and set aside.

Remove the flesh from the duck and cut it into bite-sized pieces. Place the duck in a bowl with the onion, ginger, cilantro, mint, and cashews. Pour in the dressing and toss gently.

Place the lettuce on a serving platter. Top with the duck salad and serve.

SERVES 4–6

Thai noodle salad

Dressing
2 tablespoons grated fresh ginger
2 tablespoons soy sauce
2 tablespoons sesame oil
4 tablespoons red wine vinegar
1 tablespoon sweet chili sauce
2 garlic cloves, crushed
4 tablespoons kecap manis

1 lb 2 oz cooked large shrimp
9 oz dried instant egg noodles
5 scallions, sliced on the diagonal
2 tablespoons chopped cilantro leaves
1 red pepper, diced
3½ oz snow peas, sliced

To make the dressing, whisk together the fresh ginger, soy sauce, sesame oil, vinegar, chili sauce, garlic, and kecap manis in a large bowl.

Peel the shrimp and gently pull out the dark vein from each shrimp back, starting at the head end. Cut each shrimp in half lengthways.

Cook the egg noodles in a saucepan of boiling water for 2 minutes, or until tender, then drain thoroughly. Cool in a large bowl.

Add the dressing, shrimp, and remaining ingredients to the noodles and toss gently. Serve with lime wedges, if desired.

SERVES 4

sides

Baby spinach salad

2 tablespoons olive oil
1 tablespoon lemon juice
3 cups baby spinach leaves
3½ oz small black olives
sea salt, to season

Whisk together the olive oil and the lemon juice.

Toss the spinach in a large serving bowl with the olives and the combined oil and lemon juice. Season.

SERVES 4

Red potato salad with dill and mustard dressing

6 waxy, red-skinned potatoes,
   such as portobello

Dill and mustard dressing
1 tablespoon seeded mustard
1½ tablespoons chopped dill
2 teaspoons brown sugar
3 tablespoons red wine vinegar
4 tablespoons olive oil

Steam or boil the potatoes for 20 minutes, or until tender. Remove, and when cool enough to handle, cut into 1¼-inch chunks.

To make the dill and mustard dressing, mix the mustard, dill, brown sugar, and vinegar together in a cup. Whisk in the oil with a fork until combined. Toss through the warm potatoes and season.

SERVES 4

Beet and chive salad

24 baby beets (about 3 lbs 5 oz), unpeeled,
   trimmed and washed
½ cup walnut halves
1¾ oz watercress, roughly chopped
1½ tablespoons snipped chives

Dressing
¼ teaspoon honey
¼ teaspoon dijon mustard
1 tablespoon balsamic vinegar
2 tablespoons olive oil

Preheat the oven to 400°F. Put the beetroot in a roasting tin, cover with foil and roast for 1 hour, or until tender when pierced with a skewer. Remove from the oven and peel when cool enough to handle.

Meanwhile, to make the dressing, combine the honey, mustard, and balsamic vinegar in a cup. Whisk in the oil with a fork until well combined and season.

Reduce the oven temperature to 350°F. Spread the walnuts on a baking tray and bake for 10 minutes, or until lightly golden. When cool, roughly chop the walnuts.

Combine the watercress, beet, and chives in a large bowl with the dressing and chopped walnuts and serve.

SERVES 4

Roast tomato salad

6 firm, ripe plum tomatoes
2 teaspoons capers, rinsed and squeezed dry
6 basil leaves, torn
1 tablespoon olive oil
1 tablespoon balsamic vinegar
2 garlic cloves, crushed
½ teaspoon honey

Cut the tomatoes lengthways into quarters. Place on a baking tray, skin side down, and cook under a hot broiler for 4–5 minutes, or until golden. Cool to room temperature and place in a bowl.

Combine the capers, basil, oil, vinegar, garlic, and honey in a bowl, season and pour over the tomatoes. Toss gently.

SERVES 6

Chargrilled cauliflower salad

Sesame dressing
3 tablespoons tahini
1 garlic clove, crushed
3 tablespoons seasoned rice
  wine vinegar
1 tablespoon vegetable oil
1 teaspoon lime juice
¼ teaspoon sesame oil

1 head cauliflower
12 garlic cloves, crushed
2 tablespoons vegetable oil
2 baby romaine lettuces
1¾ oz watercress
2 teaspoons sesame seeds,
  toasted
1 tablespoon finely chopped
  Italian parsley

Preheat the chargrill pan or barbecue hotplate to medium heat. In a non-metallic bowl, combine the tahini, garlic, vinegar, oil, lime juice, sesame oil, and 1 tablespoon water. Whisk together thoroughly and season.

Cut the cauliflower in half, and then into ½-inch thick wedges. Place on a tray and gently rub with the garlic and vegetable oil. Season well. Chargrill the cauliflower pieces until golden on both sides and cooked through. Remove from the chargrill pan.

Arrange the romaine leaves and watercress on a serving platter and top with the chargrilled cauliflower slices. Drizzle the dressing over the top and garnish with the sesame seeds and parsley. Serve immediately.

SERVES 4

Moroccan carrot salad with green olives and mint

1½ teaspoons cumin seeds
½ teaspoon coriander seeds
1 tablespoon red wine vinegar
2 tablespoons olive oil
1 garlic clove, crushed
2 teaspoons harissa
¼ teaspoon orange flower water
1 lb 5 oz baby carrots, tops trimmed,
    well scrubbed
⅓ cup large green olives,
    pitted and finely sliced
2 tablespoons shredded mint
1 cup watercress

In a small frying pan, dry-fry the cumin and coriander seeds for 30 seconds, or until fragrant. Cool and then grind in a mortar and pestle or spice grinder. Place into a large mixing bowl with the vinegar, oil, garlic, harissa, and orange flower water. Whisk to combine.

Blanch the carrots in boiling salted water for 5 minutes, or until almost tender. Drain into a colander and allow to sit for a few minutes until dry. While still hot, add to the vinegar dressing, and toss to coat. Allow to cool to room temperature, so that the carrots can infuse the flavors of the dressing. Add the olives and mint. Season well and toss gently to combine. Serve with the watercress leaves.

SERVES 4

Minted potato salad

1 lb 5 oz new potatoes, halved if large
½ cup Greek-style yogurt
1 cucumber, grated and squeezed dry
3 tablespoons finely chopped mint leaves
2 garlic cloves, crushed

Boil or steam the potatoes for 10 minutes, or until tender. Allow to cool.

Mix together the yogurt, cucumber, mint, and garlic and toss through the cooled potatoes. Season well.

SERVES 4

Bean salad

9 oz green beans, trimmed
9 oz yellow beans, trimmed
3 tablespoons olive oil
1 tablespoon lemon juice
1 garlic clove, crushed
shaved parmesan cheese, to serve

Bring a saucepan of lightly salted water to a boil. Add the green and yellow beans, and cook for 2 minutes, or until just tender. Plunge into cold water and drain.

Put the oil, lemon juice, and garlic in a bowl, season and mix together well.

Put the beans in a serving bowl, pour on the dressing and toss to coat. Top with the parmesan and serve.

SERVES 6

Snowpea salad with Japanese dressing

9 oz snow peas, trimmed
iced water
1¾ oz snow pea sprouts
1 small red pepper, julienned
½ teaspoon dashi granules
1 tablespoon soy sauce
1 tablespoon mirin
1 teaspoon brown sugar
1 garlic clove, crushed
1 teaspoon very finely chopped ginger
¼ teaspoon sesame oil
1 tablespoon vegetable oil
1 tablespoon toasted sesame seeds

Bring a saucepan of water to a boil, add the snowpeas and cook for 1 minute. Drain, then plunge into a bowl of iced water for 2 minutes. Drain well and combine with the snow pea sprouts and pepper in a serving bowl.

Dissolve the dashi granules in 1½ tablespoons of hot water and whisk in a small bowl with the soy sauce, mirin, sugar, garlic, ginger, sesame oil, vegetable oil, and half of the toasted sesame seeds. Pour over the snowpea mixture and toss well. Season to taste and serve sprinkled with the remaining sesame seeds.

SERVES 4–6

Cucumber salad

1 large cucumber
1 tablespoon sugar
3 tablespoons lime juice
1 tablespoon fish sauce
1 shallot, finely sliced
4 tablespoons cilantro leaves
1 small red chili, seeds removed and finely chopped
2½ oz snow pea shoots

Peel the cucumber, cut in half lengthways, remove the seeds and cut into ¼-inch thick slices.

Put the sugar and lime juice in a large bowl, and stir together until the sugar has dissolved, then add the fish sauce.

Toss the cucumber, shallot, cilantro, and chili through the dressing, then cover and refrigerate for 15 minutes. Just before serving, cut the snow pea shoots in half and stir through the salad.

SERVES 4

Salata baladi

2 tablespoons extra virgin olive oil
2 tablespoons lemon juice
1 romaine lettuce, torn into bite-sized pieces
3 firm, ripe tomatoes, each cut into 8 pieces
1 green pepper, cut into bite-sized pieces
1 large cucumber, seeded and chopped
6 radishes, sliced
1 small salad or red onion, thinly sliced
2 tablespoons chopped Italian parsley
2 tablespoons chopped mint

In a bowl, whisk together the olive oil and lemon juice. Season well.

Combine the vegetables and herbs in a serving bowl and toss well. Add the dressing and toss to combine.

SERVES 4–6

Fennel salad

2 large fennel bulbs
1 tablespoon lemon juice
1 tablespoon extra virgin olive oil
2 teaspoons red wine vinegar
1 cup Niçoise olives, pitted

Trim the fennel bulbs, reserving the fronds, and discard the tough outer layers.
Using a very sharp knife, slice the fennel lengthways as thinly as possible and put in
a bowl of cold water with the lemon juice.

Just before serving, drain the fennel well and pat dry with paper towel. Toss in a
bowl with the oil and vinegar. Finely chop the fronds, add them to the fennel with
the olives and season to taste.

SERVES 4

Warm potato salad with green olive dressing

3 lbs 5 oz small, waxy potatoes, scrubbed
½ cup green olives, pitted and finely chopped
2 teaspoons capers, finely chopped
3 tablespoons finely chopped Italian parsley
2 tablespoons lemon juice
1 teaspoon finely grated lemon zest
2 garlic cloves, crushed
½ cup extra virgin olive oil

Boil the potatoes for 15 minutes or until just tender (pierce with the tip of a sharp knife—if the potato comes away easily it is ready). Drain and cool slightly.

Meanwhile, place the olives and capers in a small bowl with the parsley, lemon juice, lemon zest, garlic, and olive oil. Whisk with a fork to combine.

Cut the potatoes into halves and gently toss with the dressing while still warm. Season to taste.

SERVES 6

Warm artichoke salad

8 artichokes (about 7 oz each)
1 lemon
½ cup shredded basil
½ cup shaved parmesan cheese

Dressing
1 garlic clove, finely chopped
½ teaspoon sugar
1 teaspoon dijon mustard
2 teaspoons finely chopped
  lemon zest
3 tablespoons lemon juice
4 tablespoons extra virgin olive
  oil

Remove the tough outer leaves from the artichokes until you get to the pale green leaves. Cut across the top of the artichoke, halfway down the tough leaves, then trim the stems to 1½-inches long, and lightly peel them. Cut each artichoke in half lengthways and remove the hairy choke with a teaspoon. Rub each artichoke with lemon while you work and place in a bowl of cold water mixed with lemon juice to prevent the artichokes from turning brown.

Place the artichokes in a large saucepan of boiling water, top with a plate or heatproof bowl to keep them immersed, and cook for 25 minutes, or until tender. To check tenderness, place a skewer into the largest part of the artichoke. It should insert easily. Drain and cut in half again to serve.

For the dressing, mix the garlic, sugar, mustard, lemon zest, and lemon juice in a cup. Season, then whisk in the oil with a fork until combined. Pour over the artichoke and scatter with the basil and parmesan.

SERVES 4

Cherry and pear tomato salad with white beans

3 tablespoons olive oil
2 shallots, finely diced
1 large garlic clove, crushed
1½ tablespoons lemon juice
1⅔ cups red cherry tomatoes, halved
2 cups yellow pear-shaped tomatoes, halved
15 oz canned white beans, drained and rinsed
4 tablespoons basil leaves, torn
2 tablespoons chopped Italian parsley

Put the olive oil, shallots, garlic, and lemon juice into a small bowl and whisk to combine.

Put the tomato and beans in a serving bowl. Drizzle with the dressing and scatter the basil and parsley over the top. Toss gently to combine.

SERVES 4

Asian salad

2 sheets nori, cut into 1¼- x ¼-inch pieces
2 tablespoons seasoned rice wine vinegar
2 teaspoons lemon juice
¼ teaspoon sesame oil
2 teaspoons canola oil
2¼ oz mizuna leaves
2¼ oz snow pea shoots
2 cucumbers, shaved
½ daikon, shaved

Toast the nori on a preheated chargrill pan or barbecue hotplate for 5 minutes, or until crisp.

To make the dressing, whisk together the vinegar, lemon juice, sesame oil and canola oil. Toss the mizuna, snow pea shoots, cucumber, daikon, and nori with the dressing and serve.

SERVES 4

Thai green papaya salad

1 lb 2 oz green papaya, peeled and seeded
1–2 small red chilies, thinly sliced
1 tablespoon grated palm sugar or brown sugar
1 tablespoon soy sauce
2 tablespoons lime juice
1 tablespoon fried garlic (see Note)
1 tablespoon fried shallots (see Note)
½ cup chopped green beans
8 cherry tomatoes, quartered
2 tablespoons chopped roasted unsalted peanuts

Grate the papaya into long, fine shreds with a zester or a knife.

Place the papaya in a large mortar and pestle with the chili, palm sugar, soy sauce, and lime juice. Lightly pound until combined. Add the fried garlic and shallots, beans, and tomato. Lightly pound for a further minute, or until combined. Serve immediately, sprinkled with the peanuts.

SERVES 4

NOTE: Packets of fried garlic and shallots are available from Asian food stores.

Radicchio with figs and ginger vinaigrette

1 radicchio
1 small curly endive lettuce
3 oranges
½ small red onion, thinly sliced into rings
8 small green figs, quartered
3 tablespoons extra virgin olive oil
1 teaspoon red wine vinegar
⅛ teaspoon ground cinnamon
2 tablespoons orange juice
2 tablespoons very finely chopped
   candied ginger with syrup
2 pomegranates (optional)

Wash the radicchio and curly endive leaves in cold water and drain well. Tear any large leaves into pieces.

Peel and segment the oranges, discarding all of the pith. Place in a large bowl with the onion rings, salad leaves, and figs, reserving 8 fig quarters.

Combine the olive oil, vinegar, cinnamon, orange juice, and ginger in a small cup. Season to taste. Pour over the salad and toss lightly.

Arrange the reserved figs in pairs over the salad. If you are using the pomegranates, slice in half and scoop out the seeds with a spoon. Scatter over the salad.

SERVES 4

Cucumber, feta, mint, and dill salad

4 oz feta cheese
4 cucumbers
1 small red onion, thinly sliced
1½ tablespoons finely chopped dill
1 tablespoon dried mint
3 tablespoons olive oil
1½ tablespoons lemon juice

Crumble the feta into ½-inch thick pieces and put in a large bowl.

Peel and seed the cucumbers and cut into ½-inch dice. Add to the bowl along with the onion and dill.

Grind the mint in a mortar and pestle until powdered. Combine with the oil and juice, then season. Pour over the salad and toss well.

SERVES 4

Warm marinated mushroom salad

1 lb 10 oz mixed mushrooms (such as baby button, oyster, brown, shiitake, and enoki)
2 garlic cloves, finely chopped
½ teaspoon green peppercorns, crushed
4 tablespoons olive oil
4 tablespoons orange juice
9 oz mixed salad leaves (mesclun), watercress, or baby spinach leaves
1 teaspoon finely grated orange zest

Trim the mushroom stems and wipe the mushrooms with a damp paper towel. Cut any large mushrooms in half. Mix together the garlic, peppercorns, oil, and orange juice. Pour over the mushrooms and marinate for about 20 minutes.

Arrange the salad leaves in a large serving dish.

Drain the mushrooms, reserving the marinade. Cook the flat and button mushrooms on a hot, lightly oiled chargrill pan or barbecue hotplate for about 2 minutes. Add the softer mushrooms and cook for 1 minute, or until they just soften.

Scatter the mushrooms over the salad leaves and drizzle with the marinade. Sprinkle with orange zest and season well.

SERVES 4

Warm choy sum salad

13 oz choy sum (see Note)
2 tablespoons peanut oil
3 teaspoons finely grated ginger
2 garlic cloves, finely chopped
2 teaspoons sugar
2 teaspoons sesame oil
2 tablespoons soy sauce
1 tablespoon lemon juice
2 teaspoons seasame seeds, toasted

Trim the ends from the choy sum and slice in half. Steam for 2 minutes or until wilted and arrange on a serving plate.

Heat a small saucepan until very hot, add the peanut oil and swirl it around to coat the pan. Add the ginger and garlic and stir-fry for 1 minute. Add the sugar, sesame oil, soy sauce, and lemon juice, heat until hot and pour over the choy sum. Season to taste, garnish with sesame seeds and serve immediately.

SERVES 4

NOTE: *Choy sum* is a popular Chinese flowering vegetable available from Asian food stores. Alternatives include *bok choy* (*pak choy*).

Lentil salad

½ onion
2 cloves
1⅔ cups puy lentils (see Note)
1 strip lemon zest
2 garlic cloves, peeled
1 fresh bay leaf
2 teaspoons ground cumin
2 tablespoons red wine vinegar
3 tablespoons olive oil
1 tablespoon lemon juice
2 tablespoons finely chopped mint
3 scallions, finely chopped

Stud the onion with the cloves and place in a saucepan with the lentils, lemon zest, garlic, bay leaf, 1 teaspoon cumin, and 3½ cups water. Bring to a boil and cook over medium heat for 25–30 minutes, or until the water has been absorbed. Discard the onion, zest, and bay leaf. Reserve the garlic and finely chop.

Whisk together the vinegar, oil, juice, garlic, and remaining cumin. Stir through the lentils with the mint and scallions. Season well. Leave for 30 minutes to let the flavors absorb. Serve at room temperature.

SERVES 4–6

NOTE: Puy lentils are small, green lentils from France. They are available dried from gourmet food stores.

Eggplant, tomato, and sumac salad

2 eggplants, cut into ½-inch thick rounds
3½ fl oz olive oil
5 large, firm, ripe tomatoes
1 small red onion, finely sliced
4 tablespoons roughly chopped mint
4 tablespoons roughly chopped Italian parsley
2 teaspoons sumac (see Note)
2 tablespoons lemon juice

Put the eggplant slices in a colander, and sprinkle with salt. Leave the eggplant for 30 minutes to allow some of the bitter juices to drain away, then rinse the slices and pat them dry with paper towel. Using 2 tablespoons of the olive oil, brush both sides of each slice, then chargrill for 5 minutes on each side or until they are cooked through. Let the slices cool slightly and cut them in half.

Cut the tomatoes into wedges and arrange in a serving bowl with the eggplant and onion. Scatter the mint, parsley, and sumac over the top.

Put the lemon juice and remaining olive oil in a screw-top jar, season and shake. Drizzle the dressing over the salad and toss gently.

SERVES 6

NOTE: Sumac is a spice made from crushing the dried sumac berry. It has a mild lemony flavor and is used extensively in many cuisines, from North Africa and the Middle East, to India and Asia.

Chickpea salad

1 lb 12 oz canned chickpeas
3 firm, ripe tomatoes
1 red onion, thinly sliced
1 small red pepper, cut into thin strips
4 scallions, cut into thin strips
2 cups chopped Italian parsley
2–3 tablespoons chopped mint

Dressing
2 tablespoons tahini
2 tablespoons lemon juice
3 tablespoons olive oil
2 garlic cloves, crushed
½ teaspoon ground cumin

Drain the chickpeas and rinse well. Cut the tomatoes in half and remove the seeds with a spoon. Dice the flesh. Mix the onion, tomato, pepper, and scallion in a bowl. Add the chickpeas, parsley, and mint.

To make the dressing, put all the ingredients in a screw-top jar with 2 tablespoons water, season well and shake. Pour over the salad and toss.

SERVES 8

Asian rice salad

2 cups long-grain rice
2 tablespoons olive oil
1 large red onion, finely chopped
4 garlic cloves, crushed
1 tablespoon finely chopped fresh ginger
1 long red chili, seeded and thinly sliced
4 scallions, finely sliced
2 tablespoons soy sauce
½ teaspoon sesame oil
2 teaspoons black vinegar (see Note)
1 tablespoon lime juice
1 cup roughly chopped cilantro leaves

Bring 5 cups water to a boil in a large saucepan. Add the rice and cook it, uncovered, for 12–15 minutes over low heat, or until the grains are tender. Drain and rinse the rice under cold running water, then transfer to a large bowl.

While the rice is cooking, heat the oil in a frying pan over medium heat. Add the onion, garlic, ginger, and chili, and cook for 5–6 minutes, or until the onion has softened, but not browned. Stir in the scallion and cook for another minute. Remove the onion mixture from the heat and add it to the rice with the soy sauce, sesame oil, vinegar, lime juice, and cilantro, and mix well. Cover the rice salad and refrigerate until you are ready to serve.

SERVES 4

NOTE: Black vinegar is a type of Chinese vinegar and can be found in Asian grocery stores.

Caramelized onion and potato salad

oil, for cooking
6 red onions, thinly sliced
2 lbs 4 oz fingerling or new potatoes, unpeeled
4 bacon slices
⅔ cup snipped chives

Mayonnaise
1 cup mayonnaise
1 tablespoon dijon mustard
juice of 1 lemon
2 tablespoons sour cream

Heat 2 tablespoons of oil in a large heavy-based frying pan, add the onion and cook over medium–low heat for 40 minutes, or until soft and caramelized.

Cut the potatoes into large chunks. Cook in boiling water for 10 minutes, or until just tender, then drain and cool slightly.

Broil the bacon until crisp. Drain on paper towel and cool slightly before chopping.

Put the potato, onion, and chives in a large bowl, reserving a few chives to garnish, and mix well.

To make the mayonnaise, put the mayonnaise, mustard, lemon juice, and sour cream in a bowl and whisk to combine. Pour over the salad and toss to coat. Sprinkle with the bacon and garnish with the reserved chives.

SERVES 10

index